Terms and Conditions

LEGAL NOTICE

The Publisher has strived to be as accurate and complete as possible in the creation of this report, notwithstanding the fact that he does not warrant or represent at any time that the contents within are accurate due to the rapidly changing nature of the Internet.

While all attempts have been made to verify information provided in this publication, the Publisher assumes no responsibility for errors, omissions, or contrary interpretation of the subject matter herein. Any perceived slights of specific persons, peoples, or organizations are unintentional.

In practical advice books, like anything else in life, there are no guarantees of income made. Readers are cautioned to reply on their own judgment about their individual circumstances to act accordingly.

This book is not intended for use as a source of legal, business, accounting or financial advice. All readers are advised to seek services of competent professionals in legal, business, accounting and finance fields.

You are encouraged to print this book for easy reading.

Table Of Contents

Foreword

Chapter 1:
Simple Copywriting Tips

Chapter 2:
The Nature Of The Offer

Chapter 3:
What Is It People Really Want?

Chapter 4:
How Do You Subtly Hypnotize Your Prospects

Chapter 5:
Things You Must Look Out For

Wrapping Up

Foreword

Success is discovered with meeting and exceeding the needs of your customers and clients. Are you asking the correct questions to meet their needs and establish success – for both you and your customer?

A successful enterpriser is somebody that recognizes how to sell. You might not love selling. You might not feel you're great at selling. You might even feel like you are an utter failure at selling. Whatever your self-justification on why you can't sell, if you wish to be really successful, you need not only learn the real meaning of selling but how simple selling may actually be for anybody to do.

How To Sell Like A Pro Online

Chapter 1:
Simple Copywriting Tips

Synopsis

Copywriting, what is it and how come it matters? Well whether or not you've discovered it, you've read a few forms of sales copy at some time or another. You could be watching a TV commercial message, a net banner ad or simply reading a magazine insert, either way its copywriting.

Copywriting is the art of selling individuals something with words most especially. If you have to do your own copy then it may be a little intimidating and for the most part it appears a lot easier than it really is.

All the same, there are a few things you are able to put into practice that will help achieve you excellent results. Here are a few great copywriting tips for novices.

Putting It Together

Don't be frightened of lengthy sales copy. There's a basic notion that the more copy you have on a page the less likely individuals will be to read it and really react to it. While this might be real in a few markets and niches, broadly speaking the more you write the better the reaction will be. Naturally this won't hold true if your whole copy fails to affect or persuade individuals, but it's still a crucial component.

The 1ST is a headline that sticks out and gets the reader intrigued in your product. You are able to make the font a bit larger and spotlight it or bold the sales copy headline. If you're working on a site I'd keep the background white and the font black. Remember this is to look professional and not have assorted colors or fonts that will make it difficult to read. The same is true if it's a sales copy to be sent out to prospective customers.

You'll need to write in little paragraphs and provide details of your business and what products you have that may peak their interest. Keep the verbal description simple and don't get over complicated in you sales copy. Attempt and write in terms that everybody may understand, don't get too complex about your service, and call attention to how it will benefit the customer in simple terms. Keep away from over hyping and bragging about your business or site, getting derogatory about your rivalry isn't good. Rather call attention to how you are able to benefit the buyer compared to the rivalry.

The final part of the sales copy ought to make the reader wish to purchase or contact your business. If you're writing sales copy on a site have a picture of your product with a concise description. This is where you'd put your purchase button or add to cart button. Your

sales copy shouldn't have any flash type banners if it's on a site. Most site visitors will click away with too many banners on the page.

Interject a little humor.

Utilizing humor and light-hearted publishing may help establish a relationship and get individuals to consider you a more believable source of info. This naturally helps with swaying the reader to do what you wish them to do, like make a sale or opt-in to an e-zine for instance.

Be observant. Individuals find situations that they may relate to funny. This is why so many stand-up comics start their jokes with, "Have you ever noticed...?" or "Why is it that...?"

Remember that wit is pain. It's sad but true that individuals find humor in the suffering of other people. Sure, it may be cruel, but what's funnier: somebody walking down the street and tripping over his shoestrings or somebody walking down the street and discovering a 20 dollar bill?

Surprise individuals! Hearing an amusing joke for the 8th time isn't very funny, is it? Be innovative and creative, putting off clichés that individuals have heard a million times.

Magnify. Writing about an event from your daily life, like cat sitting, may not be very funny, but cat sitting 6 cats while trying to clean the house for a visit from your boss may be.

Occasionally all it takes to get a laugh is to be uncanny. Surreal imagery like standing on line at the DMV behind Superman may do the trick.

Be specific. Writing "I discovered a fish in my car" isn't as funny as "I discovered a carp in my Caddy."

Re-script. If what you're writing doesn't sound funny, put it down. Get back to it later when your brain is clear.

Be exceedingly clear and concise.

If you're selling something, make it absolutely clear what it is. Keep away from being vague and general at any cost and give individuals the facts. Tell them what they get, why it's useful and why they require it (or why they ought to think they require it!). There's no other sure fire way to kill a sales copy than by getting general or distracting about what the real offer is. Remember the whole notion is to get individuals to perform a wanted action and any effort you are able to make to simplify it will assist dramatically.

Write your piece to the finish. Don't edit your draft while you write. Whatever your project, write it like you'd speak it.

Go back over every sentence and take away unneeded or ambiguous words. To communicate clearly you have to realize words may mean different things. One word may replace a phase and even an entire sentence.

The key to composing concisely is in the editing. Drop off conjunctions. Shorten sentences. Replace phrases with one or two

exact meaning words. Make certain the sentence structure is complete.

At the very least as you see how to write succinctly it's a great idea to continually expand your vocabulary. Always have a thesaurus.

Remember you're communicating points which readers are surmising with their own resources. You must be clear so flights of fancy don't stray too far away!

Establish worth.

The more you establish worth throughout your copy the better you'll be able to convert those viewers into real actions (sales, leads, and so forth.) You are able to accomplish this through being detailed and specific about what you're providing and actually offering something useful. Even if you have got a low end profit that's targeted toward a novice in a market, that still holds value to that target market so don't be frightened of building up the value of something seemingly little like a short report or downloadable software platform.

While these copywriting tips for novices center on a few of the main basic factors for successful copy it's always a great idea to do as much research as you can. If you're earnest about really getting great results from your copy then learning more of the advanced maneuvers is an awesome idea and well worth the time invested.

Chapter 2:
The Nature Of The Offer

Synopsis

A lot of businesses that sell a product (or service) mistake its "features" for "advantages" (the nature of the product) again and again. How come? Because they design features into the product. They don't, nevertheless, experience the advantages... Buyers do.

And the buyers want the advantages, not the features. So you have to deliver advantages, not features. Don't mix up the two on your sales page or presentation about the nature of your product.

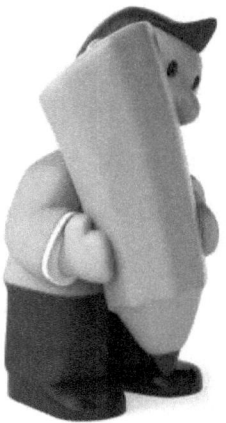

What Can You Offer

Your product intent is your product's most potent advantage, combined with a substantial, unique aspect of your business. It answers that hardest question. Why should likely buyers purchase your product, from your company?

<u>Here's how to develop this...</u>

What is it that you are selling? Put down what your product is and does.

You ought to know and comprehend each feature and benefit the product might have. Writing styles ought to always vary depending upon the desired audience. You ought to research who uses and buys the product to establish the tone and style of your audience and produce a unique voice for your product.

What is the advantage to your buyer? What trouble does it cure, or what gain does it supply?

It's frequently not adequate to simply list the features of a product as your audience might not always comprehend them. Utilize descriptive language to communicate how any one characteristic will benefit the customer and how buying the item will make their life simpler. Potential customers wish to know what the product will do for them.

What is unique about your product? About you? What makes you stick out from the competition?

Continue working on this till you are able to distinctly separate yourself from the field. There has to be a convincing reason for doing business with you, rather than your competitor. It's crucial when composing product descriptions to be concise. Utilize common language and words that are simple to understand. Clearly describe the product without becoming too technical or ho-hum so the reader remains engaged.

Summarize the above into one tight, mighty; motivating phrase that you can use again and again that will persuade your buyer to do business with you, to trade their cash for the advantages delivered by your product.

The best product descriptions always invite a sale. Be originative and encourage the likely purchaser to buy your product by telling them precisely how to do it.

As you begin to work through the above steps, you might discover this to be a lot more difficult than it appears. Don't quit!...

You must show the nature of the product. If it was simple, everybody would be making a fortune! Muster up a tight, sharp product intention that sells your likely buyer.

There's a 2nd advantage to this exercise. It will clear up your own vision of this monetization process! Write your product intention down. Keep it unwaveringly fixed in your mind.

Match your product intention to your ideal buyer's most potent motivator, either "hurting" or "something to gain".

Hurting -- individuals feel deprived, nearly all in either wealthiness, wellness, love, or happiness. Show individuals how you assist in the area that they're disadvantaged in. Make it clear that you empathize with your visitor's trouble and that you have the remedy for her hurting or fear of loss.

Something to gain -- emphasize the single most crucial favorable advantage that you offer to your buyer, in language that she will value.

If your product intention answers the "What's in it for me?" inquiry, you're midway to the sale.

Chapter 3:
What Is It People Really Want?

Synopsis

The error most human beings make is in utilizing their own values to ascertain what others want. The person who succeeds will be the one who supplies individuals with what they want.

However, to leave it at that will mean imparting your success or failure to the whimsy of blind luck. You'll merely be guessing what other people want, praying or trusting you accidentally supply it.

The secret of success is: discover what individuals truly want and help them acquire it!

Discerning Requirements

By selling what individuals truly want it converts to prompt sales for your business and in addition to that, long-term recurrent sales in the time to come for your business. You likewise establish awesome customer relationships as you frequently make them feel that you truly 'listen' to what they want and go the additional mile in supplying it to them. You're harmonized with their world and make them sense you are a reliable resource or means of assisting them to accomplish their goals and realize their ambitions.

Economically wise, being the "true supplier" to your buyers allows you to distinguish yourself from the masses of businesses who simply "get by" in the market (out of blind chance) and provides you an edge to require higher prices in the market as you understand that your services or products are constantly sought after.

You simply have to learn how to have an actual interest in and concern for others—which won't truly be hard for you as it's likewise part of human nature. Don't agree with me? Answer this: Don't you like it when somebody asks for your assistance? When you recognize a relative or acquaintance needs something, don't you try to seek resolutions for them? See what I mean? It's human nature.

Treating every individual you meet in the market whether it's on the net or person to person as a friend or relative you're helping out,

removes the need for you to put up a 'front' simply to sell something. You'll make certain what you're providing will really assist the other individual—or at the very least make sure to offer them the very best that you have to provide.

In the same way, if you know that the product or service you're offering what truly works well or would be truly beneficial to other people, why not begin by providing it to family and acquaintances instead? It's not as though you're pushing the product or service on them as you have no one else to provide it to but because you truly believe that their interests are best served by purchasing it.

What should I sell? What products are best?

These are the questions most individuals are attempting to find an answer in order for them to arrive at the definite decision. And if we truly wish to understand the answer to this question, our only choice is to do a little research.

There are all sorts of twists along the route that might lead you to believe you have a high-demand theme. We must be able to comprehend and satisfy the need, wishes and expectations of our buyers on a particular product that they're attempting to buy. These 3 are called the common needs or minimal requirements for a purchase.

Needs are the common reasons or the minimal requirements consumers are seeking in a product or service. They're called the qualifying dimensions in a buy.

Wants are the influencing attributes among a lot of choices. Expectations, on the other hand, are values or intangibles affiliated with a product or service. Expectations are in reality part of wants but they get to be exceedingly crucial when products or services are not specialized.

For instance, in studying a logic book, college students seek the following: Relevant logic constructs and use of simple language, simple to comprehend and affordable prices. These like ideas may be applied to net marketing also. After all, the Net is just a different place to sell products. The general construct of demand is the same there as it is anyplace else.

Now, the 2nd matter that has to be considered is the level of competition. Level of competition implies the ratio of your brand sales versus the overall market sales.

While companies would by nature specify its target rivals, it's in reality the consumers who in the end decide the competitive frame. We have to consequently pick out the market segment where we may have a likely leadership or at least a firm challenger role. Because the overruling aim of getting into this business isn't simply to satisfy the needs and wants of our buyers but to do so productively better than

his rivalry. Otherwise, our rivalry will wind up satisfying the buyers better than us.

3rd component to be considered is determining the basic interest level about the product. Basic interest in a product helps us to judge where our demand and rival numbers fall into the big picture.

Merely saying, if there isn't a great deal of demand for the product, and there isn't much rivalry, it would appear that it may not be so great. However the research doesn't stop here; there's one final matter to be considered. We have to also learn how other people are advertising those products. If there are a great number of them doing so, it might imply that it's a great product type to get into. Coming to the final stage of the process is studying and evaluating all the data that has been collected. We have to look at all of the information we have accumulated on demand, rivalry, and advertisement, and make decision as how they all balance out.

And here are many factors that have to be assessed: (a) not adequate demand implies not enough individuals are going to purchase (b) too much rivalry implies not enough revenue (c) a bit much advertising drives up the price of PPC ads, and rivalry also (d) not enough basic interest, blended with low demand, implies there might not be a great market even if there's rivalry attempting to make the sales.

Chapter 4:
How Do You Subtly Hypnotize Your Prospects

Synopsis

Even though the Net is an exceedingly interactional medium, it's still the terms on your web page that will make or break you.

In this chapter I'm going to share a couple of hints on how to turn your web page into a persuasive sales machine. We'll consider a couple of illustrations, and, utilizing the tips I outline in this chapter, we'll likewise come up with a list of guideposts that you are able to utilize to arrange your own hypnotizing copy to sell, sell, sell!

Grab and Keep Their Attention

The Main Question – What's In It For Me?

Your potential customer doesn't care about you. They don't have concern that you've spent $20,000 establishing the latest release of your gizmo. They don't have concern that you have a decent company logo and a neatly configured site. Nope. When anybody visits your site they have one question in mind:

"What's in it for me?"

The unrivaled purpose of your web page is to sell. And to build sales, you have to answer this query for each and every potential customer that comes to your site. The better way to answer the "What's in it for me?" Query is by relating to your likely buyers through the advantages of your product.

Characteristics VS Advantages

If your wish your web page to be an ongoing sales machine it's utterly critical that you are able to translate your products list of characteristics into advantages. Advantages sell because they appeal to individuals emotions. Characteristics don't. For instance, view this characteristic list for one particular product:

    Keyword rich URL's
    Integral contact form
    Simply add Google AdSense ads

Pretty boring, eh? Now let's translate this list of characteristics into advantages:

Keyword rich URL's: better your search engine placing by including the title of your material in its web page link. It's a long-familiar fact that all of the huge search engines prefer sites with keyword-rich links.

Integral contact form: Make it simple for your site visitors to get hold of you utilizing the integral contact form. No more messy "do it yourself" HTML forms!

Simply add Google AdSense ads: turn a profit from your knowledge and authoring skills by placing Google AdSense ad's beside your material. This product makes it easy to put in AdSense code wherever you decide.

As you are able to see, I've added the chief advantage of every point. I'm sure you'll concur that the advantages list makes the product sound much more appealing than the ho-hum characteristic list.

Social Substantiation

Next time you are somewhere, try this out:

Walk up to a corner where there are a set of stoplights. Once there's no traffic (make certain you double check), walk across the street before the walk light turns green. If there are others waiting with you, 9 times out of 10 they'll likewise begin walking. This is an illustration of social substantiation.

Here's a different illustration:

In the beginning part of a week discover a comparatively quiet restaurant and have lunch there. Rather than sitting inside, sit at one of their outside tables. Over the run of your meal I assure you at least five individuals will come into the restaurant and order their lunch on what would've commonly been a quiet day for that certain restaurant.

These are simply two illustrations of social substantiation that I've discovered. Social substantiation relies on the concept of "if he's doing it, then it has to be good, so I ought to do it also".

The best way to implement social proof on your web site is via customer testimonials or referrals. By showing your visitors that people have already purchased and are using your products or services, you eliminate most of the pre-conceived doubt and skepticism they carry about you and your company, and believe me; everyone has doubts, even for the best of companies.

Headlines

The matter of authoring a great headline may fill a book in itself. There's no correct or incorrect way to compose a headline, and you ought to always test assorted versions of your headline because if you have a feeble headline very few individuals will carry on reading, therefore resulting in lost sales.

The most beneficial way to come up with a headline is to place yourself in your potential customer's shoes. Ask yourself "If I were among my potential buyers, what terms, characteristics, advantages, etc would make me wish to continue reading and finally order my product?"

I'll give you a couple of tips to get you started out authoring or revising your own headline:

Social substantiation headlines work well. Utilize phrases like "Who else wishes to [have whatever your product does]", "Learn how 1000s of individuals have [accomplished whatever your product executes]", "Here's how to [acquire the advantages your product supplies]", and so forth.

Your headline ought to stress the top advantage of your product. It ought to be short and pertinent and ought to make people want to continue reading to learn more.

Keep away from headlines that sound too great to be true or include a bit much hype, like "With only an hour a day you too may become a millionaire in a month".

Explore. Look around the Net for headlines that snap up your attention and copy their formatting, or remember recent purchases you've made on the net and mark down the headline or web material that swayed you to purchase and utilize it on your own page.

Formalness not demanded

Any great business owner ought to think of his buyers as extension of him and his company. Structure your sentences as if you're talking to a close friend. I find that formalness in web copy, e-mail or phone conversations only bestows clumsiness, so I attempt to avoid it.

Certainly, if you're an enterprise-level company formalness is a must, but most individuals purchase from small companies because they favor personal interactions and value the attention to detail. Here's an illustration of what I like to address as "starchy" copywriting:

The new version of XYZ is ideal for e-mail marketers. It includes dozens of fresh characteristics perfect for anybody looking to begin and maintain an e-mail marketing campaign.

Flat, ho-hum, no advantages, and it doesn't speak to the potential customer. Always attempt and utilize the word "you" as much as you are able to, while refraining from utilizing your company name or references to your establishment as much as conceivable.

Here's a partial making over of the starchy copywriting:

Are you searching for an e-mail marketing answer that will step-up your income, put you ten steps before of your closest rival *and* make your customers adore you?

If so, XYZ is for you. We know small businesses like yours and have assembled an affordable e-mail marketing answer...

This is simply an easy illustration, but I'm sure you are able to see what I'm getting at. Remember, they don't have concern about you or your company. They only have concern about what's in it for them.

Bullets

It's not easy to study paragraphs of text on a screen. You have to break up your copy as much as you are able to. Among the best ways to catch the attention of individuals who merely scan over your web page is with bullet points.

Think about this paragraph:

XYZ makes it simple to manage a whole site from one location. You are able to update your web page at any time utilizing only a PC. You'll likewise save time and cash and be up and running in less than 60 minutes!

Now let's reformat it with bullets:

XYZ makes it simple to...

- Handle an whole site from just one location
- Create updates at any time, from any Net-enabled PC
- Save time and cash and be up and running in under 60 minutes

As you are able to see, it's much simpler to read a list of bullet points than a paragraph of textual matter. Did you also observe the ellipses (the three dots) that I put in after the opening sentence?:

XYZ makes it simple to...

This is a different copywriting trick you are able to and ought to utilize. It states to the reader "Hello! Continue reading, there's more info below". As a guideline you ought to utilize it to lead from headlines into your intro paragraph, as well as every three - five paragraphs, simply to keep the reader centered.

Chapter 5:
Things You Must Look Out For

Synopsis

Prior to us wrapping up, here's a list of matters to avoid when copywriting for your web page or product:

What Not To Do

- Massively big typefaces.

Do not make your headline gigantic simply because you saw it on a different web page. It's admittedly true that a killer headline will make or break you, however when you are able to read the headline from the other side of the room it's a bit much.

- Keep away from text background colors.

I'm certain you've seen text like this all over the net. Although you might think its attention catching, it's truly simply annoying and there's no proof it really works.

- Don't underscore for accent.

Underscores are set aside for links and links only. Don't underscore a point like this. It's atrocious and confusing for visitors to your web page.

- Be a man of your word.

If you assure a 30-day return policy, do it. Why not place testimonials from buyers who have had returns on your page to prove to your visitors that you'll politely honor all return requests?

From a site user's viewpoint, I'd like to tell you about a couple of my least-favorite things in sites (and I know I'm not solo here):

- Flash introductions

- Home pages that don't tell me rapidly what the product is/does
- Obscure/ambiguous/non-meaningful/non-intuitive icon names
- Puzzling navigation
- Not being able to come by what I want rapidly
- Braggart PR fluff (for example., "We're proud of our committal to customer service")
- Pages that don't bear "Home" and "Contact Us" buttons
- Pages that discuss some undefined, unstructured, anonymous group of buyers out there, but aren't directed at me
- Needing to scroll lots
- Lengthy, dull blocks of text
- Disquieting, moving pictures
- Pages where a soundtrack begins playing mechanically as soon as I get there
- Flavorless stock photos of groups of crazy busy, smiling, multi-cultural executives
- Links that aren't distinctly, obviously links
- Illegible text (for example., text that's too little, or colorful text on a colorful background, or text with a perplexing jumble of different fonts)
- Pages that don't tell me how to reach an actual individual
- "Contact Us" pages that provide only a form to send off a message but don't tell me the company's e-mail address, street address or phone number
- Registration forms that call for a postcode
- Error messages that put the blame on me (for example., "Bad Request")

Enquiry into this subject suggests that site users:

- Travel to a site with a particular undertaking in mind, and leave rapidly if they can't discover what they want.
- Glance over pages and headlines instead of reading each word.
- Wish to feel that they're doing something dynamic (for example, clicking) instead of just passively reading.
- Shift rapidly from page to page, pulling out only the most crucial info on every page.
- Wish to feel involved.
- Have a poorer attention span than when reading hard-copy text.
- Have confined tolerance for scrolling up and down, and detest scrolling left and right.
- Skip over flash introductions.
- Don't inevitably enter your site via your home page.
- Travel around your site in ways you didn't anticipate and can't control.

Remember... Before you compose a single word, you have to be clear about the purpose of your page. Who's it directed at? What are their percepts/motives/aspirations/goals/needs? What do you wish individuals to accomplish and experience when they visit your page? What is the picture and personality that you wish your brand to project? What are the most crucial jobs that visitors come to your page to achieve (that signifies crucial to them, not you)? What info do they require/need?

Wrapping Up

Want to understand how to promote intuitively? Simple. Become your buyer. What would make you feel great about buying your product or service? All right, that's your beginning place.

When you turn into your target market, you're on the correct path. See your product or service from their eyeballs and formulate your campaign to fit their needs.

- Once you market, provide your audience the message that they wish to hear.
- Produce content that makes your target audience feel great, not only about the product or service, but about deciding to purchase it.
- Keep your marketing in line with your moral values.
- Listen more to your gut feeling and less to outside marketing-guru content.
- Center on what makes individuals feel great about your product or service?

If you're marketing a beauty product, you help individual's look and feel better, if you're a lawyer, you assist your clients through hard situations, and you resolve troubles. Keep with that mentality, whatever your business is. The most beneficial marketing is feel-good marketing provided through effective storytelling.

PR all comes down to telling a commanding story that engages the readers, spectators or listeners and causes them to assume action.

And so, begin thinking about your marketing, advertising and PR in this way. Realize that your job is to exhibit your product or service by telling a commanding story with a call to action.

Back away and see your business from this view. Begin to make a list of your most commanding stories. You're seeking success stories.

How do you assist your customers or buyers, how do you affect their lives? Do you make their lives simpler, more gratifying? Remember, you're not selling your product or service; you're selling an experience, an emotion.

You have to let your buyers know why they have to purchase from you. If you don't tell them, they won't understand and the most beneficial way to tell them is with your winner stories.

If you have a really narrow or particular target audience, say adult female over 40, then come up with winner stories that demonstrate how you meet their requirements.

If your target market is less specific, say it's a nutritionary supplement that may be utilized by individuals of all ages, then dissect your target market into sections and come up with particular stories and messages that are contrived specifically to meet the requirements of those markets.

Once arranging your marketing plan, drill down and drill deep. You wish to make your buyers feel great about their decision. You wish them to feel they've not only made the correct conclusion, they've made a bright conclusion.

Remember, every individual who sees your PR, ad or marketing campaign has to feel that you're talking to him or her specifically.

You need your buyers or clients to feel that you configured your product specifically to meet their certain needs. So, have a look at your present promotional campaign. Now turn into your buyer. What would make you feel great about making the buy?